Nancy!

Live your life!

Love your life!

I LIKE *that* story

INSIGHT AND INSPIRATION FROM THE HEARTLAND
FOR THE FIRST TWENTY-FIVE YEARS OF LIFE

Jeff Gould

AUTHOR JEFF GOULD

Aug 30, 2021

Jeff Gould

AUTHOR
Jeff Gould

EDITOR
Clara Jacob

ILLUSTRATIONS
Alix Brennan

DESIGN
DonnaMæ Wirtjes

PRINTING AND BINDERY
Anderson Brothers
4525 41st St, Sioux City, IA 51108

PUBLISHING COMPANY
Make Design Publishing
308 E Vera Lane, Brandon, SD 57005

ISBN NO# 978-0-578-45619-5

Insight and Inspiration from the Heartland

Book One

INTRODUCTION

I wish you could be there.

Not for the tears or pain, of course.

As someone who meets with families to help plan funerals, I see the raw emotions of heartbreaking loss.

As a eulogist or celebrant at what has amounted to hundreds of funerals, I must figure out how to conduct a service that will bring a measure of healing to families who have lost loved ones.

I'm told I do a good job. I seem to have a gift for finding things to celebrate and things that offer comfort.

But I also see the truth.

Maybe I should say Truth, because most of us are pretty good at giving the world a version of ourselves that we find more suitable.

But in that room where the families gather, the masks slip a little bit, and I can see what is underneath.
What I see is what this book is about.

When people share stories they reveal information that's very helpful to me. Because I am not as emotionally involved as the family, I can step back and think, "That was a good idea." Or perhaps, "Oh…that was a bad idea."

Later on, I change a bit of each story so that only the truth remains.

And when people hear the story they say the most powerful word in the English language: "Hmm."

That "Hmm" means a story was heard. A lesson hits home. Like a small seed, a thought is planted and I can almost see it begin to take root.

Listeners commonly nod and after a pause say, "That's a good story."

These stories are too important to be called entertainment. Their price is dear enough to make me cautious in my approach. In many cases, lives were literally lost to bring you these stories.

Listeners commonly nod and after a pause say, "That's a good story."

. . .

Having said that, I must also say that the stories in this book have changed my life. I am a different person because of these stories and I believe you will be too.

These are stories for you, from people who have faced the same decisions and trials that you are facing now.

I hope you learn from their wisdom. And I hope you understand what it may have cost to bring it to you.

table of contents

swiss army knife

Go to a sporting goods store and ask to see some of their Swiss Army knives.

The big thing you'll notice right away is how many clever little things are packed into hidden recesses of each knife and the reason Swiss Army knives are handy to have around.

And you are much more intricate, clever and handy than a Swiss Army knife. Who knows what things you will discover about yourself as you move through life?

disclaimer

When I was a kid watching the cop show, Dragnet on TV, I would recite with the announcer.

"The story you are about to see is true. The names have been changed to protect the innocent."

With these stories I went a little farther. The stories on these pages consist of truth and are actual lessons from real life events—many of which surround the most painful of emotions—the loss of a loved one.

To honor and protect these families, I have changed more than names. I've also changed ages, circumstances, job titles and outcomes. I've added details that are pure fiction and I've molded two stories into one, all in an effort to protect these families I have come to love.

In doing this, I realize I may have fabricated someone that resembles a person or circumstance that is familiar to the reader.

If that is the case, I apologize and can say with complete confidence that all stories and people are fictional.

DRAGNET

FRIENDS

The Worst Possible Hug

I say this book is about lessons from dead people. In this case there were two at the same time.

I used to be a lifeguard which was a really great job for a 19-year-old kid. I stood on the shores of Weaver Lake and watched the sun set and the little kids swim. The glare off the lake was brutal, but I found a pair of cheap sunglasses that helped. Someone asked me if they were polarized, which meant nothing to me, so all summer long my irises were tricked into opening wide and letting the damaging solar rays in. That's probably why I got glasses so soon after that. Oh well.

Anyway, this is about the dead people, so on with the story. If they told us once, they told us a thousand times—never, never, never, save an actively drowning person. Reach. Throw. Row and Go. Reach first, from the safety of land. Throw a floating thing for them to grab onto. Row a floating thing out, and only as a last resort were we to Go swim to save someone.

. . .

"A drowning person is a very, very dangerous person."

"And let them drown." This statement puzzled us, but the instructor was persistent and the point was hammered home. "A drowning person is freakishly strong and will overpower you. If you can, you must let them drown to the point of absolute exhaustion or they will pull you down with them."

Then he started showing the slides. Pictures and diagrams of husbands and wives, brothers and sisters, boyfriends and girlfriends who were all dead at the bottom of a pool or lake, each hugging each other around the neck.

"This is how virtually all double drownings occur. Someone is in trouble. The second person, a friend or family member, jumps in to save them. The drowning person, in panic, kills them both."

He stopped and looked around the room at the lifeguards-in-training.

"A drowning person is a very, very dangerous person."

It took me years to figure out all the ways people can drown and all the ways that they drag friends and family down with them.

LIFE LESSON

Saving someone may require more energy, talent or ability than you have.

. . .

It took me years
to figure out all the ways
people can drown
and all the ways
that they drag
friends and family
down with them.

FRIENDS

Frank and Bill and the Why Not

Frank and Bill got out of the service and were working side by side, swinging hammers for a construction company. Frank was telling me the story more than 50 years later:

"It was after the war and things were booming. Bidding a job was easy. You added the cost of materials to the cost of labor plus 15 percent. My buddy Bill looked at me and said, 'Why not us?' And I said, 'Why not?"

"We lived by the Golden Rule and we put that on the business cards and at the bottom of each contract. Eventually we split, he went into commercial, I went into housing. He made a name for himself and God bless him, but I never wanted that kind of stress.

"I was building homes on spec in 1968 when the market went soft. Nothing sold and I had six houses sitting empty when Bill suggested I just rent 'em out, so I did. Turned out I made more money doing that then I did selling them, so that's when I switched."

Frank is telling the story and I'm doing the math, but it doesn't seem to add up. He looks about 60. Too young to have served in WWII, but later when he gives me his birthdate I realize that he is one of those rare ones that never seems to get bogged down with age. He has a twinkle in his eye and is wearing a pocket t-shirt and carpenter pants. He sits behind a beat-up desk in a room that wouldn't win any interior decorating contests, but is neat in a worn sort of way. A bachelor's place, I think. His wife passed a few years ago, but I doubt that she was ever a part of this room. A stack of paper sits on the edge of the desk, and a linoleum pad with a monthly calendar sits in the middle of the desk next to a rotary dial phone, one of those heavy black rubber kind you see in the movies. He leans back in a padded steel office chair on wheels and the springs creak.

"Anyway, that's what I do. I look around for a house or property. I pay cash for it. My buddy Oscar is a realtor and we do a lot of business. I come in low, offer cash right now, and I usually get it.

. . .

"He made a name for himself and God bless him, but I never wanted that kind of stress."

"Once I buy it, then I spend a year fixing it up. When it's done I rent it out. When I get to 12 houses, I sell the first one, usually to the people who rent it from me. So every year I buy a house and every year I sell one."

The neighborhood we're in is definitely working class. Frank tells me he named the street back in 1949. Easy enough to do, since his was the first house. He still lives in the house, it's the one I'm sitting in, the one with original decor and a beat-up desk. It's not my business to ask, but I bet he's a millionaire many times over. Even more rare, he is a millionaire who seems genuinely happy.

I ask him what house he's working on now.

"Just finished my last one." He looks content. "I'm 89 and it's time I slow down a bit."

I ask him what house he's working on now.

. . .

"Just finished my last one." He looks content.
"I'm 89 and it's time I slow down a bit."

the power of tangents

The best way to understand that forward often means sideways or backwards is to watch a crowd disperse from the lobby after a concert or play. I've done this hundreds of times myself. My wife is a choir teacher and often the very last person to leave, so I've studied the process.

Some dash out in front—often missing the finale or final minutes of the game. The need to be first is more important than mere entertainment.

Most shuffle along mindlessly following the person in front of them, not really paying attention, allowing the flow of the crowd to dictate direction.

Others bull their way through the crowd pushing people aside, not really caring if they cause damage, deaf to criticism.

And others, usually children, slip through the gaps in the crowd, sideways, backwards, a quick step here, timing an opening there. They get where they are going, seeing the whole thing like a game, emerging ahead of others usually by a circuitous, seemingly random route.

Reminds me of Frank.

FRIENDS

Al and His Back-Stabbing Friends

Al was a kind and gentle soul. He hung out at the local watering hole, always quick to share a beer and a story. Lots of nights he would pour himself behind the wheel and creep slowly home. Not a big deal since it was a small town and he only lived a few blocks away.

Towards the end of his life, he would have to crawl up his sidewalk, because he had a prosthetic leg that was of no use when he was drunk. His kindly neighbor lady would keep an eye on his house to make sure he got safe inside, especially when it was really cold outside. Another kindly neighbor would make sure that his pension check got cashed and would deliver the money twice a month.

And so on.

These kindly neighbors slowly watched him kill himself because they were his friends and it was none of their business. Now I should admit that in their spot I would probably do the same thing. I mean, what you do with your life is none of my business, right? In fact, I can be very tolerant of other folks' behaviors, especially if it takes little or no effort on my part.

But love is different from tolerance. Finally, his daughter and son-in-law and some people who really cared about him arranged to have an intervention. The doctor was there with the facts and laid them out on the table. "Al, you've had a stroke that almost killed you. The next one *will* kill you. You will need to stop drinking or you will die."

But love is different from tolerance.

Al listened in disbelief. He looked around the table at all those who loved him and were looking out for him. His eyes focused on the doctor for a full minute. Then with tremendous force he pounded the table in rage.

"No! You WILL NOT tell me what to do! I will drink as long AS I WANT TO!"

There was a shocked silence. The intervention was broken. Al turned his back on those who loved him and went back to the bar. I was at his funeral two months later. They buried him in the casket with his closest friend—a can of beer.

REALITY CHECK

Not all of your friends are your friends.

parting shot

I regularly visit a 21-year-old man in prison.
Tad is an amiable person but there is a wariness in his eyes.
It's the look of a kid who was fooled and knows it.

I told him I was writing a book of advice for people
under 25 and asked him if he had any.

"Advice? Me?" He shook his head. I changed the subject
but a few minutes later he brought it up.
"Advice? Here's something for you."
He looked at me with an expression
of bitter memory.
"You are who you hang with."

FRIENDS

The Crab in the Barrel

Pretty much every port city has a tourist area, a fishermen's wharf, and you can see this little trick played out every day. The observation is not mine. I don't know where I heard it first, but it is an important lesson about friends.

At the wharf you'll see the fishermen selling their fresh-caught wares. Fish, oysters, lobsters and more and they're in a big barrel which you can see is half full of writhing fresh-caught crabs.

You look closer—they're pretty active all right. You ask the fisherman if it might be wise to put a lid on the barrel so they don't escape.

He chuckles, "They won't. Their friends make sure of that." And then he walks away.

Curious, you stay and watch the barrel, as an especially aggressive crab gets purchase and starts crawling up and out to freedom. Inches away from certain escape, another crab reaches up and grabs on to the first.

And pulls it down.

Still curious, you watch the second reach up and make it past the first, only to get pulled down by another and another.

And so it goes—until they are all taken home and eaten.

LIFE LESSON

Sometimes the best way to leave is alone and unannounced.

. . .

Don’t get pulled down.

FRIENDS

All My Friends are Dead

I hear this comment a lot. I'll be talking to someone in their 80s and they will give me a mournful look when I ask about activities in which they are involved. Then with a sigh they will say, "All my friends are dead. I'm the only one left." Which makes me think of my wife's grandfather, Bob.

Bob is an outlier: a man who doesn't fit the pattern of what we expect from people.

For example, he decided to become a pilot when he was 72. And Bob walked everywhere. He didn't even have a car until he was in his 50s, which is hard to imagine in these times. But he and his wife had seven children, which meant they didn't have much money, and one of the ways they saved was by not having a car.

When he was 90, he gave up his car and started walking again. His night vision was troubling him and he didn't want the temptation.

• • •

He was a walker—he walked everywhere, didn't have a car until he was in his 50s, which is hard to imagine in these times.

He was one of the few people who knew each of my daughters by name. Most people shrug and say, "I know their names begin with the letter M…," like that's the answer that will give them a passing grade. Grandpa Bob knew their names though, and spent time with them, got to know each of them—when he was in his 80s and 90s.

These are just a few of the reasons he was unusual. One of the most important reasons I saw first-hand at his funeral. I was one of the eulogists. In the front row, off to the right I saw a young man I didn't recognize. He was in his late 20s and he was crying.

I talked to him afterwards and asked him why he came.

"Bob was a friend of mine." They were members of a service club and this young man was the president, and they'd become pretty close.

So, if I am doing the math right, Bob became friends with a man who was born when Bob was 76.

That could happen and probably should happen more often. People could get in the habit of continually making friends their entire life, but most people don't. Why?

IN A NUTSHELL

The best way to make a friend
is to be a friend.

friend investments

Friends are a different kind of investment but follow the same guidelines as financial investments:

Invest in friends that are diversified.
Plan on keeping them for the long term.
Choose ones that are stable, growing
and pay regular dividends.

FRIENDS

Ugly

By the time I met him, he preferred to be called by his real name. Who could blame him? He worked at a packing plant, was part of the union, did a lot of stuff in the community. But everyone at the plant called him Ugly.

I didn't know this at the time. I was talking to him at a public event when I heard a younger guy call out, "Hey, Ugly!"

The man stiffened ever so slightly then smiled, "That's what they call me," as though it was a big joke to him, too.

I looked at him. "Really?"

He nodded, pretending it was nothing. "At the plant they would do that. Big Bill Johnson would give everyone a nickname and it stuck."

I found out he worked at the plant for 40 years. That's a long time to be called Ugly.

Listen, I don't care what the benefits are, or the pay, or the job security, but the day your "friends" start calling you Ugly (or whatever demeaning name they use) should be the day you start looking for another job.

. . .

That's a long time to be called Ugly.

FRIENDS

The Land of Misfit Toys

The gym where I go every day…well, almost every day…okay, three, maybe four, days a week is not the finest place with the greatest equipment, but it has guys I'm used to and I imagine it's where I'll keep going, God willing.

There's a guy with a broken elbow that sticks out at an odd angle while he does curls. There's a smallish woman with a pony tail and covered with tattoos that runs, runs, runs, always on the same machine and never talks to anyone. There are three guys that look like refrigerators—they might be on steroids, or it's possible that they earned all that meat—who are at the gym easily three hours a day. There's another guy who does random workouts with very heavy weights, shouting out equally random things to no one in particular.

"He's harmless," someone assures me. The word harmless doesn't seem right, but it is. They look intimidating, all of them, but over time you come to find out some stories that make them just people.

Curt is tall and loud and intense. You'll see him talking smack to others in the gym or complaining about a piece of equipment or another guy who is wrecking the equipment. Like I say, he's loud.

. . .

They look intimidating, but over time you come to find out stories that make them just people.

But he's also very open. He'll tell you about his dysfunctional family, ticking off the members, "I got two brothers who are alcoholics. I had three, but one killed himself. My sister did the same, she was into pills. My parents were both alcoholics."

The more he talks the more you realize just how many demons are chasing him. His lower lip is distended from a very large glop of chew. Not good, but it looks like he has done the best he could, picking addictions that are the least damaging.

And so we all hang out here, not really together but together nonetheless. Kind of like a bar but with better choices and outcomes. I could get a home gym but it won't work as well. I like coming here because it helps me and it helps me help others.

FRIENDS

The Mover

I think his name was Roy. He had lived in more than 23 towns by the time I got to meet with his family to discuss his funeral. That's a lot of moving. Yet his family did not seem the worse for wear. In fact, they seemed a happy, well-adjusted lot that spent time talking about the various joys, calamities and humorous events they had been through.

Mom would move us in, put up curtains and a few knick-knacks from our childhood and 'bang,' we were home, no matter where that was.

And Dad would join us up in something. I mean, he was crazy about it. He'd move to town and start asking about the best groups to join. He'd join the most active service group. We'd start going to the church that was most involved in the community. He'd ask around looking for the best coach and join us up in whatever sport he coached.

Then he'd come home and we'd sit at the table and he'd talk about how lucky we were to see so many great places and live in so many great communities and how this was going to be the best place ever. And then he'd have a barbecue, invite the neighbors over and see what kind of friends he could make. He was good at it, but we could see how hard he worked at it, too.

"He would say, if you want a friend, be a friend." And it seems corny, but we believed it. We really believed that we had it better than other kids. I guess we still do."

. . .

"Mom would move us in, put up curtains and a few knick-knacks from our childhood and 'bang,' we were home."

FRIENDS

Five Close Friends

I'm stealing this exercise from a friend of mine named Jim Rieffenberger, which proves he's a friend because he's okay with it. It works best if you use it on a younger person.

Take a deck of playing cards and deal out five face down, a set of five for everyone who is playing the game.

Then you'll say, "You will have only about five close friends at any given time. And it has been proven that you will become the average of these five closest friends. Income, status, happiness—pretty much every measurable factor can be matched with these five close friends. Such is the power of friendship. Now before we flip the cards over, let's use these cards to describe what your friends are like.

"Aces are low and so are these friends. They gradually get better, the higher the value: a two is better than an ace, a three is better than a two and so on. A 10 is the most excellent of friends—helpful, supportive, fun, a real quality person that everyone looks up to.

"Far worse than the aces are the face cards. These are not really your friends; they are frenemies—people who are steering you down a path for their own personal agenda and not yours.

"The jack is a weak person always asking for help, never giving you any back. His value is a negative two. A jack is needy and complaining—the world is bad and they blame you for it, they need your help to do projects, they need to borrow your car, your money, your free weekend. They never return the favor and make you feel guilty every time you are with them.

"The queen is the bad girlfriend or boyfriend. Her value is negative five. Queens are even worse than jacks because they are using the emotions of love or the passion of sex for their own selfish purposes. Your parents or family are most concerned about the queen and the queen knows it. For this reason the queen will try to put you in a spot where you must choose.

"The king is the worst of all. His value is negative seven. He has the power of charm and charisma. He is cunning and gets his way. Others follow him and he can stand up to the people who have persecuted you in a way that earns your loyalty. Sadly, he uses that loyalty to make you do bad or even illegal things. In your heart of hearts you wish you never knew him, but he is the king and he rules your life.

"Now flip your cards over and look at them. These are your friends for life. Add up the value of each and average out the numbers. This is now your value and it is the value you will have for the rest of your life.

"Of course, we know that life is not really like that. People grow up and move, friends come and go. So now, take your five cards and draw from the deck. Keep the best five cards you want and discard the ones you don't want. Do this all the way through the deck. When the deck is finished, you are now an adult. Now average the cards. This is now who you are.

"What has changed? Why has it changed? Friends are friends through loyalty. But loyalty is often used by harmful friends to hold you back or damage you. Always look for good friends among people you admire. Always be on the lookout for people who are using you under the guise of friendship."

Play this game with a younger person and watch their perceptions change. Watch your perceptions change.

FAMILY

The Double Deadbeats

Esther was about 85. She called because she was worried about paying for her funeral. She had a few insurance policies but they were borrowed against up to the hilt and she was certain that her children would be unable to handle the emotional and financial hardship.

I arranged to meet at her home because her granddaughter was borrowing her car.

"Can we meet in the early afternoon, say 1:00?" she said. "My shift doesn't start until 4:00 and that will give me time to get to work."

I arrived at the appointed time. A man was sitting on a sofa in the living room watching TV at full volume. "Darryl, can you turn that thing down?" said Esther. Darryl was unresponsive, so with a sigh, she led me to the slightly less noisy kitchen table where there was a plate of mostly uneaten food.

"Darryl, you didn't finish your hot dog."

Darryl heard that all right. "Because I hate hot dogs, you know that! Why didn't you pick up a pizza like I told you?"

"I don't get paid till Friday, and that's what I could afford!" said Esther.

Darryl did not respond; he just sulked at the TV.

She nodded to the couch and whispered, "He's been that way since Gretchen moved in. That's my granddaughter."

"The one who is borrowing your car?"

She nodded. "She needed to visit some friends and said she'd be back in time for my shift."

"Does she drive you to work?"

The older woman looked puzzled. Like the question had never occurred to her. "No."

Then I got to the sad reality. It seemed that Esther had worked all her life and even that very day was due to work 4:00 pm to close at a nearby McDonald's. Yet she had no money.

"I have a life insurance policy, but I borrowed against that to fix Darryl's car. I'd managed to put a little more aside by picking up some weekend shifts, but since Gretchen needed a place to stay, that's been costing me more, too."

"Do either of them work?"

Esther shook her head, "Darryl struggled ever since he was little, so I've been taking care of him."

I looked over at Darryl. He was wearing sweats and a basketball jersey and his hair was gray. I put him at about mid-50s. He looked okay to me, but I didn't know the whole story.

More of the story walked in about five minutes later when a younger, grumpier, more feminine form of Darryl walked in.

"You're almost out of gas, Grandma." Then louder, "Turn that sh** down!" She went to the fridge, opened it and rooted inside. "Where's the Diet Coke?"

She got the same story about payday that Darryl got and gave a similar response. She flopped down on a recliner near her dad and started complaining about the show he was watching.

I looked at Esther slumped at the table, oblivious to the argument in the background. She reminded me of Shel Silverstein's *The Giving Tree*. She looked at me—85 years old and getting ready to work an eight-hour shift.

"I just don't get it. I worked hard my whole life. What happened?"

WHAT HAPPENED?

LIFE LESSON

A child will never learn to walk
as long as you're willing to carry him.

the real purpose of chores

If a kid can walk, he can help out. If he's two years old, he should have two tasks that should take no longer than two minutes.

When he's three, he should have three tasks that take no longer than three minutes. This, by the way, is not a time-saver—not at first. It would be simpler to do it all yourself.

But if you are to prevail, you must, with good cheer, swoop into a room and say, "It's time to clean your room. You pick up your toys and I will make your bed. Some day when you are big enough, I will let you make your bed by yourself" (child psychology does work). You also have to wait for him to compete the task, which will seem like a tedious waste of time.

If you do this every day, you will eventually have a 10-year-old who will clean his room, cook meals and take out the garbage. I've seen it happen.

Interestingly, these kids also seem to be happier than the ones with no chores.

FAMILY

The Potato Pickers

Words have different meanings to different people, even common words like "home."

When Jim was eight, and his older brother was 11, they ran away from home. For six months. It wasn't a pack-a-handkerchief-with-sandwiches-and-be-home-by-nightfall escapade. No, their escape was well-thought and far-reaching.

I was never told why they felt the need to get as far away from home as possible. All I know is that these two little kids rode a passenger train as far west as they could until they ran out of money and then kept hitchhiking until they ran out of food. They made it as far as a potato farmer's house in Idaho.

It's hard to imagine those days—strange little kids alone on a train, then showing up at an unknown farm looking for work. How is that even possible? Maybe it was more common back then or maybe the farmer really needed the labor.

Anyway, they dug potatoes for that farmer for six months until, for reasons that were not explained to me, they went back home.

The end of the story surprised me.

There was no tearful reunion—a joyous father welcoming the lost. No calling the authorities to cancel a nationwide search. In this story, the father beat the older boy senseless but did not touch Jim.

Which might explain why Jim resented his father after all those years and why the brother resented Jim.

WELCOME TO IDAHO

THE TAKEAWAY

A home must be a place where you feel safe, or it is not a home.

your home is a castle—literally.

Your home is where your family retreats to after a day of battle out in an often dangerous and hostile world. It is a place where you discuss what happened:

"What was the best thing that happened today?"
The answers are celebrated around the table.

"What was the worst thing that happened?"
The wounds are then bound with bandages of love and sympathy.

Then after an evening's rest and rejuvenation, the warriors leave the castle, ready to face their foes.

If your home is not a castle, scars of fear and insecurity cripple your family even into future generations.

FAMILY

Leon and the Lost Boys

Leon was in his late 80s, a tough old bird. When I was talking to him he was upset about everything. He was mad at the government, the economy, his limited pension, and probably most mad that his health was failing and no one was listening to him like they did when he owned and ran a gas station off the interstate.

His wife showed me a picture. In it Leon was a tall drink of water with black hair and a top to bottom uniform with stripes down the pants and sleeves—the kind that service stations issued in the late 1950s.

I asked about his life. He told me about his time in the service and then opening the station after the war and about his no-good wife.

"She was a drunk!" Leon spat the words. "I told her to fix herself or get out. I came home and she was drunk, so I threw her out!" There was no remorse in his eyes, even after all those years.

The woman at his side came along a few years later. She was the one trying to smooth things along, trying to keep him on track.

It came time for me to get family information. "When somebody dies, people want to know who the family is and where they are."

She listed the names of the children they had.

LIFE LESSON

The question isn't if your parents were good. The question is, were they good enough?

"Anyone else?"

"The boys," Leon said. He gave their names and ages. This was the first time I figured out that when he threw his first wife out, he threw his two young sons out as well.

"What are their names?" Before he could answer, his wife patted his arm gently and said, "They're not going to come, Leon."

That sentence hit hard, I could see it. He slumped a bit in his chair and a light went out of his eyes.

A light that spoke maybe of a future meeting, a reconciliation perhaps.

His voice was now empty. "No, I suppose not."

The rest of the meeting was different. Leon sat smaller in the chair, no longer interested in what we were talking about. The seeds of a long-ago sown wrath were just now being harvested.

He left and I typed up his information and wondered about his boys. At some future time, they may happen to look up his service folder information. If they do, they will see his biography. And if they search for the names of children, theirs will not be listed. I wonder how they will feel.

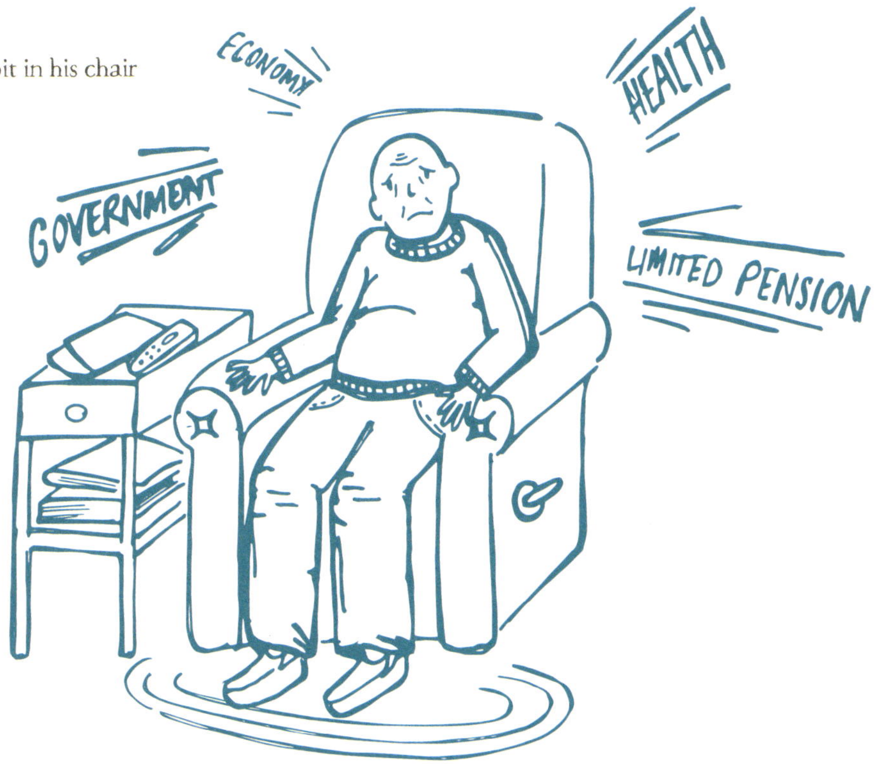

FAMILY

Jon and Jerry and Joyce

Joyce had died. She was in her early 40s, but looked quite a bit older. Her sister was there trying to piece things together. She was two years younger but looked equally worn down.

It was a sad story and hard to say where it all started to go wrong. Joyce came from a pretty rough childhood and started hanging around with some pretty rough people. One of those rough people was a guy who figured out how to take advantage of her loneliness and left her with a baby and not much else.

Being alone with a baby is hard for a poor, single mother—lots of long nights and no money and few chances to be young again. Well, she should have known better, but I can't say I'd have done differently in her shoes. She got pregnant again and now had Jerry and Jon to take care of.

. . .

It was hard to say where it all started to go wrong.

She did not finish school, got jobs where she could—usually convenience stores, day labor or fast food—always for minimum wage. Her sister was in the same boat and the two of them limped along together, offering a couch to sleep on when there was an eviction, giving a ride to work or school if there was a car that worked or a schedule that allowed it.

Talking to Jerry and Jon was an experience in anger, despair and sorrow. Both wore black clothing, not because of mourning, but because that's what they wore. Shirts with skulls and tattoos of skulls and eyes that burned with the injustices of a life that they were dealt.

I tried to think of something to say. I don't recall coming up with anything worthwhile. Afterwards, a classmate of Jon's said that he didn't go to school much and when he did, a group of boys sought him out and beat him up. There was no intervention, no calling out the bullies.

Jon eventually dropped out, and the school authorities wrote it off as a dysfunctional family.

Which I suppose is as good an answer as any.

CAUTION AHEAD

The greatest hazard of sex
is having a child you are not prepared to care for.

. . .

Being alone with a baby is hard for a poor, single mother—lots of long nights and no money and few chances to be young again.

FAMILY

Walter, the Dutiful Dad

Walter got married young. He and his wife had kids right away, quite a few. And so his dreams of college were done—he had new responsibilities.

He took a job in town working at a factory. He didn't care for it but he didn't complain. Instead he'd say something like, "It puts food on the table." Or else he would shrug and say nothing.

. . .

"I did what people wanted me to do."

Walter was not a smiler, not at all. In fact, he was a frowner. He had a wrinkle between his eyebrows that was permanent and his lips pulled down into a scowl.

He was dutifully active in his church and dutifully active with chores around the house. His wife should have been happy with the arrangement, but she frowned a lot, too. His kids did well enough in school and as soon as they were able, they fled the house to go off into the world.

I asked Walter about his life and his answer was short: "I did what people wanted me to do."

His wife was next to him and I wondered if the comment was meant for her. If it was, she did not flinch that I could see. Their feud had settled in for the long duration.

This…duty…was a common theme in Walter's life. He'd express it in small, pointed ways—an audible sigh, a newspaper rustling, turning a deaf ear to a question or comment.

What's eating THAT guy?

A mutual acquaintance asked me later, "What's eating that guy?"

I had a theory but wasn't sure if I should share it. But it turned out I didn't have to. A couple of months later he died of cancer. He was in his 60s but looked 20 years older.

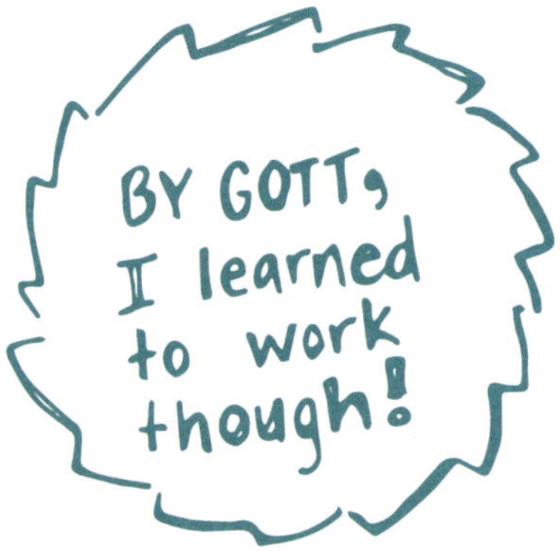

FAMILY

Hard-Headed Germans

I have seen it at least 20 times.

An older guy, named Otto or Klaus, will be talking about his father, another German named Otto or Klaus, and how mean he was. Beltings, beatings, shouting, never a kind word, just work, work, work. Sunup to sundown.

There will be an edge to his voice and usually a lesson, "By Gott, I learned to work, though!" I'll throw out a comment like, "Well, I guess they had a lot of pressures keeping the family fed," trying to add a little perspective.

He'll scoff and shake his head. "The old man was just an ornery cuss." Then he'll talk about his own tough life trying to make ends meet, caring for his children and providing for his family.

And when his children are discussed it is usually with a measure of disgust based on the children not living up to his high work standards.

“Do they know that you love them? How much you care for them?”

The question catches him off guard. He’ll look at me with an expression between suspicion, surprise and disdain.

“What?”

And so the cycle continues.

LIFE LESSON

Before you commit, meet the family.
It will predict what you're in for.

the family huddle

In a football game there is always a huddle. That's where the play is called. After the play, the players get back to the huddle to communicate what they know and to find out what the next play is.

The dinner table is where the family huddles. Family members find out how the day went, celebrate victories and commiserate about defeat. It's where family jokes are remembered, and where memories are made.

The more a family eats together, the more success the children will have in life.

As you plan for this in your future, remember: Don't invite your TV to the table—it's not part of your family. And using your minivan as a dinner table as you drive from practices to appointments may feed your family food, but it doesn't feed much encouragement.

FAMILY

The Fried Chicken Pastor

This guy was in his late 20s, full of optimism and energy. I don't know where he is today. I only met him once and that was more than 20 years ago.

He was reminiscing about his own childhood. His dad was a Baptist preacher and he had seven brothers and sisters. When he talked about Sunday it was with a plain, childlike delight.

"We did not have much money. We would pitch in where we could, with a paper route or babysitting, to bring money home to help out my mother and to see the look on her face…" He smiled at the memory.

"Anyway, between school and jobs and helping around the house, we were busy, busy people until Sunday." He smiled again, eyes closed.

"But the best part was after church."

"Saturday night, we'd help my mom cook and pack a big basket of fried chicken and biscuits and whatever kind of fruit we could find," he said.

"Sometimes it was fresh, other times baked into a pie. Then we'd head off to church all in our best and sit in the front pew and watch my dad preach his sermon. That was great."

He continued, "But the best part was after church. We'd pile into the station wagon and head off to the swimming hole and all day long we'd splash and play and eat and nap and wake up and do it all over again."

As he remembered the story, his excitement was infectious. He really did seem to have a great childhood.

"So that's part of why I am a pastor now. First of all, I feel like I'm called to it. Second, it just seemed like a great way to raise a family."

At the time we had just started out our family. We had two little girls and I was looking for some advice.

Maybe that's why I remember the story so well.

FAMILY

The Pink Warrior

I've grown to recognize the power of fashion. Within moments of meeting someone, a split-second decision is made, and what you're wearing has a lot to do with that.

And the woman I met, who I'll call Rose, had done everything right.

She was not dressing like a younger person—a classic mistake. Nor was she dressed for comfort—another mistake. (Older people must look for every advantage to avoid being ignored, and comfortably dressed older folks are seldom noticed.)

Rose wore cream-colored slacks and a matching leather vest and purse. Everything else was a light, dusty pink—her blouse (with sleeves turned up at the cuffs), her shoes, even her hair had a tinge of pink.

Her jewelry was gold—bracelets, watch, necklaces and rings.

As a husband and father of four daughters I can tell you this ensemble took at least an hour to put together. But as I said, if you're in your 80s and want to get even a little bit of respect, this is the price you must pay.

Rose had enough of that certain *je ne sais quoi* that I wondered if she might have a lesson or two to teach. I asked her what advice she'd give someone in their first 25 years of life.

"Me? Oh, no, don't ask me about my first 25 years."

That's when I learned a few things.

She grew up in a strict religious community. When Rose was six, her father announced to the family that he was leaving them for a woman and was moving to California.

This community assumed Rose's mother was to blame. The family was forced out. With no car and no money, options were limited.

They moved to a town about 15 miles away from the community. This new town was also very religious, but at least the persecution was diminished somewhat. (Relatives of the husband were as venomous as they were numerous in the old place.)

Rose's mother managed to get a room in the hotel in town. The 15' by 15' room contained a bed, an old-fashioned kitchen range, a toilet and not much else.

For three years they lived there. Rose's mother found work as a mechanic, and the kids walked to school and were avoided. "People said hello, but not much else. I was never invited to a birthday party, or event or over to play," she said.

The only spot of warmth in that cold little town was the smile of the town librarian, who introduced her to Zane Grey *(Riders of the Purple Sage)* and then to other authors and other worlds. "I loved to read and I don't really remember ever being sad."

The dad came slinking back and, after three years, the mother was worn out enough to take him. And that was the gist of Rose's pretty bleak childhood.

Grit or sand or guts or whatever Zane Grey might have called it, this woman in her 80s had it, with plenty to spare. She only offered the details because I asked.

She shrugged. "Everybody has setbacks."

WORDS OF WISDOM

It's not where you start, it's where you finish.

Be a Pink Warrior.

CAREER

Bob and the Sweet Gig

Bob was an okay student. He knew how to work hard, had a dad who knew a guy who knew a guy and, because Bob was a pretty strong kid, he got a job right after high school working construction, making a wage of…wait a minute.

If I tell you what he made, you wouldn't get it because it was a long time ago. Instead, let me ask it this way: If you were 19, what would be an hourly wage that would make you think, "Wow! Why the hell would I continue busting my ass in school?" Because that is exactly what Bob thought—so he took the job.

Was that a mistake? Well for Bob it was. You see, he didn't really like the work, so he'd dead-head it through the day, waiting to punch out. To make the days more bearable, he purchased a GTO—a completely tricked-out muscle car, bright yellow. The payments were expensive and the insurance was more so, but the job he hated covered it, so he kept the job he hated to drive the car he loved.

It was 30 years later when I learned Bob's story. His back was shot. Construction is hard on body parts. Bob had three surgeries and was getting shots in both knees because the cartilage was wearing down. He was about 60 pounds too heavy and diabetes was creeping in.

. . .

He kept the job he hated to drive the car he loved.

His wife harped on him and he complained about his job. The one bright spot was his new extended cab Silverado, tricked out with every bell and whistle.

How do I know this stuff? Like I said, I work at a funeral home. In the case of Bob and his wife, they're discussing a parent. But as they talk I hear more than they realize. I admire the truck; it's parked outside, still with dealer plates.

I open my mouth to ask how much it cost, but I change my mind. I already know it was very, very, very expensive.

LIFE LESSON

Never take a job only for money.

the why game

Many of the people we admire are rich.

But wealth is best acquired when it is an afterthought, a result of living a life of passion. If you never get rich, but still live a life of passion, who cares about the money?

Play the Why game to see what I'm talking about. Pretend you're a five year old, always asking your older self the question, "Why?"

I want a lot of money.
Why?
So I can get a nice car.
Why?
So I can drive it.
Why?
So I can have fun.
Why?
So people will look at me and smile.
Why?
So I will feel accepted.

When you play the Why game the answers usually boil down to acceptance, security, peace or contentment. And none of these require earning a lot of money.

CAREER

The Dead End

Some of my stories come second-hand. A number of years ago, when we were just starting out in life, my wife was having a conversation with another woman about her job. My wife had just become a teacher and the woman was quizzing her about her job choice.

"I knew I wanted to be a teacher when I was 10. I loved music, playing the piano and singing. I didn't really have the best music teacher, to be honest, and I thought that maybe someday I could change that. From that moment I knew who I wanted to be."

"It must be great to have a calling like that." The other woman sighed. "My job is so stressful. More of a grind, really. You are so lucky to have a job where you feel like you are making a difference."

Libby looked surprised but didn't say anything.

The woman heaved a sigh and checked her watch. "Gotta go. Another long day."

She adjusted her white coat, stuck her stethoscope into a pocket and headed out of the examination room.

is it a job or a calling?

If you're on the fence about whether you like your job, stop calling it your job. Refer to it as your calling.

If that seems a little far-fetched, remember this:
Some folks in every occupation love their job, no matter what that job is.

"When I pick up people's garbage, I keep the neighborhoods clean and stop the spread of disease. I am important."

"If I do my job right, the numbers tell the correct story and can help my manager make a better decision. I am important."

"When I patch potholes, I keep the roads safer for all the families who travel on them. I am important."

With a little thought, any job can be experienced as a calling.

When your occupation is your calling, you do it better and with more intention and purpose. You also care about it more and are more likely to be called into another opportunity when it arises.

That's why it's your calling.

CAREER

The World's Oldest Millennial

As long as there have been young adults, there have been older adults complaining about them. When I hear that Millennials are unrealistic in their job expectations, I smile and think about a job interview I once had.

I had just graduated from college with a mediocre grade point average and absolutely no idea what I wanted to do.

To add salt to the wound, I was on crutches after knee surgery and was living in my parent's basement. There was a recession at the time but for me it was a full-on depression (definition: it's a recession if you have a job and a depression if you don't).

I sent my completely generic resume out to companies who sent it to their HR departments who would scan it over for its obvious flaws and dump it in the round file. I would call them, leave a message and never hear back. It's a story as common as dirt.

I did happen across one lucky break when I got an interview at a giant pharmaceutical company. I happened to be in a good mood that day and struck up a conversation with a guy walking in with a briefcase. Turned out he was

. . .

It looked like a fancy prison.

the manager and a nice guy.

He interviewed me for a position in pharmaceutical sales. I could tell he liked me. I nodded my head earnestly and spoke of my fervor for both pharmaceuticals and sales. I was asked back for a second interview where I sat with a circle of other applicants, each trying to respond with polite interest to what others were saying while at the same time trying to muscle them aside with a better answer.

I made it through that barrier and was invited to a third interview. It was the same guy with the briefcase I'd met earlier! We talked about some of the exciting things the company was coming out with and what a great career opportunity it was.

Then after a pause, he looked at me and said, "You don't really want this job, do you?"

I looked at his brochures and the pictures of the Eli Lilly campus and what amazing things a career like that offered. I had never thought about working in a shiny box made of windows that looked out over a parking lot of shiny cars on black asphalt. It looked a lot like the place my dad worked. It looked like a fancy prison.

I slumped a little in my chair and looked at him.

"No."

Most people don't start out living their dream because they don't have a dream yet.

IN SUMMARY

Your first job helps you figure out what yours might be.

. . .

I had never thought about working in a shiny box
made of windows that looked out over a parking lot full of shiny cars.

CAREER

The Switcher

You couldn't help but like Marv—at least I couldn't. He had about a million stories to tell and, as you can see, I'm a sucker for stories.

Marv's stories were mostly about his checkered employment career. He was about 60 when I met him, full of energy and still with a bit of the rebel in him, which was apparent in each of his stories.

For example, he'd been an airline mechanic. "Makin' good dough!" he whistled long and low. Then he'd talk about some part of the industry, sharing a little shady, behind-the-curtain stuff—which was unfair in his eyes—and then would come the punch line: "So I said, 'Screw it.' Walked off the job."

I was a good audience at the time—in my mid-20s, kind of naive when it came to business and wide-eyed at the thought of just leaving.

"You mean you just walked away right then?" The story had involved a plane stranded with broken hydraulics, passengers on the tarmac and a pushy boss demanding that he put in the extra hours and fix it. I could figure out the pushy boss but I wondered about the stranded passengers.

"Damn right I did. You should have seen the look on that SOB's face."

I asked if that ruined any chances for future airline employment.

"Screw 'em." He waved his hand with the nonchalance of a guy who knew there were plenty more jobs where that came from.

And I heard about them. He had a repair shop (crummy business, no way to make a living), sold auto parts (the territory was ridiculous, they had him traveling across four states), sold printers (they kept screwing with his base), construction (work a guy to death!), print sales (all the good clients were taken by the bleeping boss's son)—and so on.

His resume must've been four pages long by the time I met him. At that point he was selling radio advertising. And I couldn't help but notice that he liked to talk to me about selling advertising more than he did talking to clients and actually selling advertising.

He had a nice wife who was quite a bit younger than he was plus a young daughter. The wife had an anxious look about her, like she was afraid he would walk away from this job, too. For his part he did nothing to relieve her worries, saying if he didn't get a better client list he'd walk.

I liked him (he was as close as I ever got to knowing a rogue) and I was kind of worried about him, too. "You want to keep working the rest of your life?" I asked.

He laughed. "Damn right! I will work until I'm shot to death in bed by a jealous husband."

It didn't work out that way. He, like Elvis, had a massive heart attack (apparently some people mistake the signs of a heart attack as a call from Mother Nature) and, like Elvis, he died on the throne. It was a sad end to a life that had far too many beginnings.

LIFE LESSON

You never get a good job until you get good at a bad job.

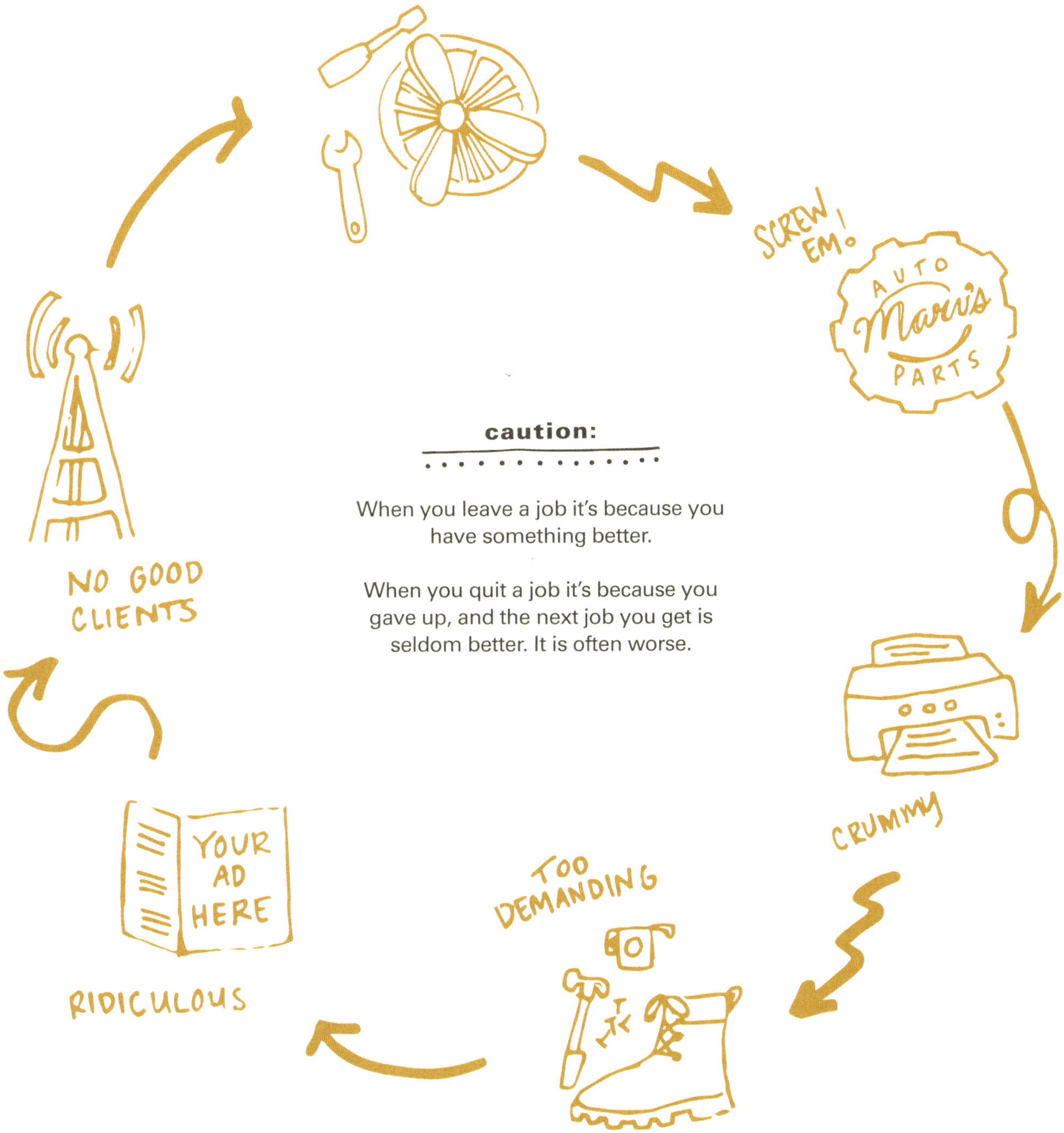

caution:

When you leave a job it's because you have something better.

When you quit a job it's because you gave up, and the next job you get is seldom better. It is often worse.

CAREER

The Wounded Vet

Roy was a veterinarian somewhere in his late 60s but looked about 20 years older.

He walked with a slow shuffling gate, his eyes in a perpetual squint, maybe because of years in the sun, maybe because of physical pain.

He was a large animal vet who spent decades climbing in and out of pens, corrals, farrowing pens and milk parlors, dealing with very large, not necessarily kind animals in all kinds of horrible weather.

Many of these animals had marked him with permanent souvenirs of their displeasure. And the job's continuous and repetitive hand motions had left his hands crippled into semi-permanent claws. The weakened hands made many doubtful of his abilities, so farmers and ranchers would call around looking for younger, stronger vets to handle the business.

But when the younger, stronger vets wouldn't answer the phone late at night, on weekends and during holidays, Roy still would. He'd get a call and drive as far as 70 miles in the middle of the night, often at the end of a 70-hour work week.

Because of those extra hours, Roy had lost his license three times—not for drinking, but for falling asleep at the wheel.

It wasn't fair. Despite his years of service, Roy was no longer respected by his colleagues. He became an object of ridicule.

When asked about retirement, he shook his head stubbornly. "I am a veterinarian," he said.

. . .

But when the younger, stronger vets wouldn't answer the phone late at night, on weekends and during holidays, Roy still would.

REMEMBER

Your occupation is not you.
It is a temporary thing that describes part of you.

career hazards

Every career has hazards. Some are physical hazards, where joint decay, hearing loss, varicose veins or injury are inevitable.

Other careers heighten mental stress, leading to increased incidents of depression or even suicide. Statistics say the average person switches careers five to seven times in their life.

Maybe that's a good thing.

CAREER

The Unsatisfied Sailor

I met her at a high school reunion. Not mine, my wife's. If that ever happens to you—getting dragged along to a high school reunion—you have two choices. You can either be bored stiff around a lot of strangers or you can start asking questions and see what you learn.

I struck up a conversation with Pam who was the VP of an education firm. A day or so later, I asked my wife if she was valedictorian or class president or captain of the basketball team. My wife shook her head. As far as she could remember, in high school Pam was a quiet person who played an instrument in band, but that was all. I tell you this so you understand where she started from.

After high school Pam didn't have a plan, so she joined the military. In the Navy, because she was young, she was assigned to a computer task that no one older or with higher rank cared to do.

After she learned the computer work, she was told to teach what she knew to these same older, higher-ranking men—who were cranky and wanted nothing to do with computers. It was not easy work, but she liked the challenge of getting obstinate people to learn, despite themselves—to see a glint of understanding and interest in the eye of a man who was learning but didn't want to admit it.

After a few transfers Pam found herself in Omaha where there were no more opportunities in the military. At that point she had a husband and kids and was back where she started with no real idea of what she wanted to do with her life.

Well, not quite.

She remembered that feeling she had when teaching others. So she went to school and got a degree in teaching physical education. And no one was hiring. Pam got her certification in English and found that, again, no one was hiring. She was told that there was an opening for math teachers, so she got another certification and this time she got a job in the Omaha school system as a math teacher. For a while.

She found an opportunity at a private company as a math tutor because it seemed like it was better. Eventually she moved into management, because that too seemed better.

Not quite satisfied, Pam took a position as a manager at another company specializing in teaching English to foreign students.

In time she was offered a position in Hawaii (by the way, when you are "offered a position," it means you can negotiate a pretty good salary, because they want you more than you need them—and that's a good thing) which worked until she was offered another position, this time to work out of her home in San Diego.

That's where Pam was at the time of our conversation—a conversation that led me to believe that she liked the job but was still not quite satisfied.

I realized that her professional life had now gained a momentum that was pulling her into greater and greater circles.

I looked around the room full of other people her age that had not done as much professionally as she had and asked her if she knew why.

She said, "No, I don't. I see it as completely random."

I nodded, but wasn't quite satisfied with her answer.

LIFE LESSON

A satisfactory job is only satisfactory to those who are easily satisfied.

• • •

Completely random
or the perfect plan?

RELATIONSHIPS

Sunni and Dani

Sunni was living in England when his dad asked him to go to visit relatives in India.

"What for?"

"I want you to meet someone."

Well Sunni knew where this was going and was not going to have any part of it. Arranged marriages are part of Indian culture and parents will spend long hours discussing the good and bad points of potential spouses.

This was exactly why the young bachelor had moved far away from traditional India to the cosmopolitan West. But his dad was paying for the trip. What could be the harm in a free vacation?

• • •

It was more than a coincidence or con.

Sunni's idea of a risk-free vacation looked all the brighter when he arrived just in time for a nationwide rail strike and, with a certain smugness, Sunni approached the ticket office and asked for a ticket to a certain village to meet a certain girl he had never heard of and was certain he would never have to see.

The man at the ticket counter turned to look glumly at a destination board full of cancellations. Except one.

With disbelief, the teller checked the destination again. "You're in luck!" he cried. "In all of India, that's the only train running."

Four days, and countless impossible coincidences later, Sunni found himself engaged to a beautiful young woman he had just met, after a meeting arranged by the families, sight unseen.

I met them about 40 years after that day. They laugh at the story. Sunni still tells the tale like it was some kind of trick he got conned into. Dani says nothing but shoots me a dazzlingly beautiful smile that makes me think it was more than a coincidence or a con.

When they talk, their conversation weaves back and forth. It's pleasant to hear because of the undertones of respect and love that are evident.

RELATIONSHIPS

The Dorito Diabetic

Ellen, Kate and John all went to the same high school. Kate was pretty and started dating John in high school. They became a couple and got married.

Ellen dated some men but, for reasons that make sense only in the passing of time, never did marry.

Kate became a nurse, John got into construction work, and from a distance Ellen heard about how things fell apart.

It was not that John was a bully or a mean man—he was just a bad husband. He never consulted with Kate over purchases large or small. If Kate ever questioned his spending, he would only shrug.

He had his own hobbies that involved his own friends, never her or her friends. Probably worst of all was his health.

• • •

He's digging his grave with his teeth.

In his early 40s, John was diagnosed with diabetes, a condition that made him even angrier and more stubborn. Not only would John not follow any sort of diet, but he refused to take any medication. And his eating would make a seventh-grade boy sick.

While he watched TV in the next room, Kate would hear John unwrapping and eating Slim Jims, Oreos, Little Debbies and Doritos with melted Velveeta singles over the top.

I heard a phrase once: "He's digging his grave with his teeth." It's an excellent description of John's behavior. Despite Kate's pleading, or maybe because of it, John continued to do whatever the hell he wanted until he finally died as a result of his uncontrolled diabetes and stubbornness.

His funeral was sad. He was not very old. And despite of their differences, Kate was sad as well.

Kate's family thinks since she's still so pretty, some single doctor will snatch her up. But I've heard through the grapevine that Kate is done with gambling her life on husbands and will stick with being single, thank you very much.

I visited with Ellen recently. She said, "I always thought it was unfair that I never met someone or got married. All my friends did. But as the years have gone by and we get together, I hear all the stories…"

She paused. The words she said next seemed to surprise even her.

"Maybe I got the better deal."

BE CAREFUL

You can marry more misery in twenty minutes than you can earn in a lifetime.

book shelf

THE FIVE LOVE LANGUAGES:
THE SECRET TO LOVE THAT LASTS By Gary Chapman

This book has been around since 1995,
so you've probably heard of it in passing.

Women should read this book and keep a copy on their shelf at all times. Men should read this book, too, but never admit it.

The gist of it is that people show their love in different ways and surprise, surprise, the genders seldom share the same language. For example; folding the laundry is just as important to some people as a dozen flowers or a candlelit dinner. Reading this book won't save your relationship, but it will give you a couple of tools that can help—if you use them.

RELATIONSHIPS

The Kitchen Set

Whenever I saw the couple, Lyle was always joking and Harriet was always laughing. He was what they used to call "hail-fellow-well-met"—a guy who could enter a room with a shouted greeting and then work the room with jests and jokes, Harriet in his wake.

About six months after Lyle died, I met with Harriet, telling her that not all marriages were as happy has hers had been.

She sat very quietly and then said in a low voice, "Lyle was not a very good man."

Harriet seemed divided between loyalty and honesty. "He was always joking with others, but at home his jokes were mean and he would yell if he did not get his way."

She spoke just above a whisper.

"I only wanted a kitchen set."

"My mother had inherited some money when my father died, about $9,000. She said it was for me to do what I wanted with. But Lyle had other ideas."

"I only wanted a kitchen set." The phrase brought back memories of Sears catalogs and TV game shows, when the grand prize would be a dining room table, six chairs and a china cabinet.

(After I met with her, I searched Google for "Kitchen Set 1950" and found old catalog photos. The most expensive set I could find was $850.)

Harriet continued, "One day, Lyle came home with a big semi-truck. He was going to get into hauling livestock and he'd taken my $9,000 to put down on the truck."

Her shoulders slumped a little more. "That didn't work out so well. After a couple of years, I didn't see the truck. When I asked about it, he would get angry and yell."

Her shoulders slumped even more and she shook her head slightly, once to the left, once to the right.

She looked up with real remorse: "I only wanted a kitchen set."

LIFE LESSON

A bully can be easy to date, easy to marry, but hard to recognize. Look for the signs early.

beware of the bully

"You complete me" is a dangerous thought. You complete yourself.

This is hard work that is barely even started by your middle 20s. The more you are comfortable with yourself, by yourself, the less likely you will fall for the controlling wiles of an overbearing (and sometimes charming) bully.

RELATIONSHIPS

The Lady in the Lincoln

I used to work in a cemetery. Most days I found an excuse to walk the grounds. If that sounds creepy, it isn't.

It was a memorial park which means all the markers are flat to the ground. It was more than 80 acres in size and on most days I spotted a bit of nature that made me smile. It might have been a hawk overhead, a heron wading through a pond or the sunlight framing tree branches in a certain way.

Sometimes I saw a lady that drove a Lincoln. She looked at nature too, only she motored through the park with her window down. One day we happened to meet. I was on foot and she was in her car, pulled off on the side of the road, watching some ducks in a pond.

We struck up a conversation about the weather, which is something Midwesterners do. I asked who she was here to visit. She gestured over her shoulder.

"My husband."

Here's a tip: When you find out someone has lost a loved one, don't change the subject. If you do it makes it seem like the deceased was not important or that the person's memories aren't worth asking about.

. . .

When you find out someone has lost a loved one, don't change the subject.

I found out his name was Ron and that he died seven years earlier. "What did you like about him?"

Her answer came after a moment of consideration. "He was dependable."

"Dependable?"

"Yes. He was always there for me."

A good answer but maybe not what I was expecting. While I was thinking about her answer, she gave another one.

"And he believed in me."

"What do you mean?"

"He was eight years older than me. Shortly after we were married, he gave me the checkbook and said, 'From now on, I'd like you to take care of this for us.'"

We talked a bit longer. Then she continued on her way, motoring along, window down. I thought about what she said. A marriage can succeed or fail for many reasons.

The fact that she still came to visit his grave weekly, even seven years after his passing, meant theirs had been a success. And from our conversation I knew that their successful marriage was based on at least two humble qualities: dependability and trust.

But did it work?

Well—she was driving a Lincoln.

DATING TIP

Watch very carefully how your date talks about his or her parents and treats the waitress.

the certificate

It is literally a piece of paper and an optional ceremony.

Yet study after study proves that a marriage certificate increases health, lowers stress and improves the odds of staying together. If you really love someone and want to stay together—get married.

RELATIONSHIPS

Great Grandma in Stilettos

As you've probably gathered, I attend a lot of funerals. And whenever I can, I take a look at the memory boards. These collections of photos and memorabilia are usually displayed at funerals and visitations.

They are fascinating—like reading history books, only more interesting: faded Polaroids of camping trips; formal portraits of weddings or military service; cracked black and white snapshots of men standing next to a new car, women in hats and gloves squinting into an Easter sun.

If you get there when the family has time to talk, you can usually get a pretty good story to go with each picture.

• • •

"Put your tongue back in your mouth, buddy. That's your great grandma!"

For example, at a recent visitation I saw a small black and white photo of a young woman in dark shorts and a white sleeveless blouse. She was leaning back on the grass, bare-legged. One lithe leg was stretched out while the other bent at the knee and on both feet she wore open-toed stilettos.

Her hair was dark and curly, flowing over her trim shoulders. And she was smiling in a way that said she was beautiful and she knew it.

I pointed to it and remarked, "Nice shot."

The man laughed, "My 15-year-old son saw that yesterday and said, "She is hot!" I said, "Put your tongue back in your mouth, buddy. That's your great grandma!"

On the same memory board were many other pictures of the same woman. The most recent photos show her with sagging arms, a double chin, many wrinkles and grey hair. The smile is the same, but that's about it.

Later on, someone pointed to the first picture and said, "This is what you buy," and then to the second, "…and this is what you get."

LIFE LESSON

Real beauty is more than skin deep.

. . .

They say you can't tell a book by its cover. But I say that you probably can.

It's true. Every memory board either has a beefcake picture of a shirtless kid with clear eyes and a smile, standing relaxed and carefree, staring into his future, or in the case of great grandma, a little bit of cheesecake.

These photos are often more worn out than the others, no doubt given to a boy or girl a long time ago, a memento of the prime of life, the giver unaware that it is the finest picture that will ever be taken of them, that physically she or he will never look that good again.

They say you can't tell a book by its cover. But I say that you probably can. Using the advantage of looking back, I can tell you that the guy who looks like a devil-may-care hell-raiser in the early picture pretty much turned out that way his whole life. These guys tend to die in their 60s or 70s, the cigarettes and drinking taking their toll, so when they die they seem older.

The women are harder to judge. By and large their appearance in later life seems to have more to do with who they spent their life with. The ones who pick a steadier type seem to last longer and hold up better. They have more pictures, too, maybe because there's more to be happy about.

When I ask about spouses, I have to do it carefully. It can be a loaded subject. Generally speaking, I say nothing about marriage at all, figuring if it was a good union, they'll bring it up with a smile and a lot of stories. If they never bring it up, it's a sign of something unhappy.

Sometimes I have no choice because I need to ask who will attend the service. I'll ask the adult children, "Will your father be attending?" Or, "I see no mention of your mother, is she still alive?"

The looks between the children tell the story.

MONEY

Alvin, Who Owned a Sports Franchise

I change all the names in these stories, even though almost all of the folks I write about are dead. I especially have to be careful about Alvin because he owned a sports team.

Owning a sports team seems like a license to make money, but there is a big risk. Any student of sports can think of numerous professional leagues and teams that were started up, promoted and then failed for any number of reasons.

Well, Alvin hit the motherlode. He and his brother took a risk and bought a franchise. They hung on tight until the network broadcast money came through and by the time I visited him he was rolling in money.

And misery.

His kids had moved away and seldom visited because Alvin was crabby, demanding and suspicious.

I spent a few hours with him over the course of several visits as he put money aside for his funeral and I figured out that he was mainly lonely. He didn't trust his kids to have any interest in him besides his money, and because there was a messy divorce in his past (he traded their mother for a stylish younger model, much to his honest regret), he may have been right.

I do remember his kids being on edge, trying to be kind and patient to the crotchety old guy—they sure didn't want to be left out of any inheritance. After one appointment, one of the children pulled me aside and said, "Thanks. I thought for sure he'd blow his lid over this."

I felt sorry for the old guy. I called him up a few weeks later and asked if I could visit.

"Why?"

"I don't know. I thought maybe you could use the company."

"No." His voice was tinged with suspicion. For all he knew I was after his money, too. That's the tough part about money. Once you have some, you can never be sure if people like you or your money. And it makes it tougher to talk to them—I mean, can you be sure that your motives are 100 percent pure when you're being nice to an old millionaire?

You wouldn't think so, but he reminds me of the young man I visit in prison. Tad is about 21, has a couple of amateurish tattoos he got on the outside and some really elaborate ones he got on the inside. His cellmate is a murderer, in for life.

When I visit with him, his eyes constantly dart around the room. He knows who the dangerous people are and he keeps his head on a swivel. He's in for three more years and there's a chance this will be his first and last stay. How I met Tad and why I visit him is another story for another chapter but suffice it to say he is happy for the company.

We play cribbage and talk about stuff, big and small. We visit in a bland, carpeted area under the eye of a prison guard. I can't imagine what I could pass over to him, considering the security, but I know that after we meet he will be strip searched anyway.

Tad is in a dangerous place. He is lonely and never suspects me of any ulterior motive. Despite the humiliation of a strip search, he is glad to see me. His prison is stark and harsh. Alvin's house was the finest that money could buy. But make no mistake—they both were prisons.

BEWARE

Money does not buy happiness. It provides only limited security and has no relationship at all to happiness.

=72

the rule of 72

This is very handy for figuring out what it costs to borrow money.

THERE ARE MANY NUMBERS THAT MULTIPLY TOGETHER TO REACH 72.

8 x 9 = 72

6 x 12 = 72

36 x 2 = 72

Easy, right?

Well, these numbers will tell you how long it will take to double your money at a given interest rate.
Money at 6 percent interest will double in 12 years (6 X 12 = 72).
Money at 12 percent will double in 6 years (12 X 6 = 72).
This also helps you estimate how much money you'll pay in interest.
If you have a 10-year loan at 7.2 percent interest, you'll pay double what you borrowed.

MONEY

Boot Money

Justine was named after her father Justin, a farmer who read *The Wall Street Journal* and had a sharp mind for figures. He also trusted his namesake, sending her off to college at the age of 16 (she graduated from high school early) with a single check for the entire anticipated four-year-cost of her college degree!

Do the math and calculate what that check might equal today and ask if any 16-year-olds you know would be up to the task. Well, she was. She graduated from college a bit early and joined her new husband in a military barracks in Germany where, as newlyweds, they used their saving and budgeting system called Boot Money.

The system was simple. The Army paid once a month. They paid their bills and then divided the rest. Most went into the right combat boot for the end-of-the-month expenses. The rest went in the left combat boot for long-term savings. This was an uncommon system among their peers.

Most GIs spent the money fast and quick. Bars, pubs and restaurants were packed the first half-week of the month. But, by the third week, the money from the right boot got them a quiet evening and immediate service any place in town. Using money from the left boot, Justine was able to buy a Pfaff sewing machine of indestructible quality. When Justine and her husband returned to the U.S., they used this Boot Money philosophy to pay off their house in less than 15 years and to fully fund the education of their children. It was a mostly-wise use of money that serves as a mostly-wise example of how to live.

I say mostly-wise because years later they planned to visit Germany again after the kids grew up. They certainly had enough money in the boot. But the trouble with Boot Money is its desire to stay in the boot. They never did go back to Germany; there was always another future day for doing something so frivolous.

When Justine was diagnosed with a terminal illness, her husband had plenty of money to spend on the disease and no time to spend on the vacation.

LIFE LESSON

Rich people are rich because they learned how to handle money when they were poor.

the 20/4/10 rule

No child can learn to walk without falling. When it comes to figuring out how to handle money, expect to stumble and bleed. A good bit of the bleeding comes from figuring out what you can afford to drive or not drive.

The 20/4/10 rule is a fast rule of thumb to figure out the kind of transportation you can afford:

20: Buy something when you can put 20 percent down.

4: Make payments for no more than four years.

10: The cost of your car (gas, insurance, payments, maintenance, etc.) should not exceed 10% percent of your gross pay.

This may be easy or hard depending on what you make. If you're starting out, it's tough. If you have a loan on a car, even if it's a beater, you may still be required to carry full (expensive) auto coverage while you're making payments. Your insurance payment may even be bigger than your car payment.

Do the math. Maybe you can't afford a car at this stage of your life. It's hard to imagine, but many people born in the 1930s talk about not having a car growing up. I remember talking to a woman whose 30-year-old mother was widowed with five children. "The first thing she did was sell our car."

Back then it was possible to walk everywhere. Today Uber and Amazon may make car-less life possible again.

MONEY

The Curse of the Instant Millionaire

A buddy of mine is an investment advisor who happened to run into instant millionaires looking for help. These people were the ones we all envy—folks who beat the astronomical odds and won the lottery!

In this case it amounted to $4 million after taxes. Nice!

Even nicer was that this windfall landed on a quiet couple of modest means that were in early retirement, squeaking by on social security and a modest pension. What a difference a sensibly-invested and carefully-spent $4 million would make during their golden years.

Wrong.

About a year after their windfall, I brought up the subject to my buddy. He shook his head in dismay.

"They are blowing through it at a tremendous pace. It will be gone in about a year and a half."

What? How could this prudent, middle-class, retired couple do this?

Because it was free.

For example, they had a son in a bind (a chronic condition for this kid). He had run into some trouble, and now he was getting back on his feet. He had managed to get a job working nights but needed a way to get to work.

Was there any way they could buy him a car? Well, in the old days, the couple would have bought what they could afford, a beat-up car to get the kid through.

The newly prosperous couple bought him a brand new car, even though they were hesitant.

He had a poor driving record so insurance would be expensive. The job was in a sketchy neighborhood and they were concerned about him parking a nice vehicle in a bad area. In truth, they suspected the new car would wind up like the others he had driven in the past: battered, dented and neglected.

Why did they make this admittedly dubious purchase? Because they had the money.

This simple "free money" philosophy multiplied by hundreds of similar decisions meant they would be broke again within two years of getting $4 million.

They are not alone. Statistics show about 70 percent of lottery winners are bankrupt within five years.

MONEY TIP

If you earn money you keep it.
If you get money, you can't.

book shelf

THE RICHEST MAN IN BABYLON
By George S. Clason

This is actually a series of booklets written by George S. Clason in the 20s that were distributed by banks to their customers. Each story in the book is a fable about how impoverished tradesmen of old learned secrets of wealth and money management from wise old merchants.

They're easy to read, and the principles are simple. If risk-tolerance matrices and balanced-portfolio discussions bore you, but you like reading stories, you'll find this a painless way to learn money management lessons. I wish I had read this book when I was 20.

MONEY

The Prigge Place

Farms are not named after who owns them. They are named after the people who *used* to own them. The family that farmed the 80-acre section of land called the Prigge Place was the Bachmans. They bought it from the Prigges 30 years earlier, but it remained the Prigge Place until Joe Webster bought the place in 1981.

You would think it would then be called the Bachman Place, but that does not always happen. It's possible neighbors will still call it the Prigge Place decades after the Bachmans are dead and buried.

Oh, well.

Buying family farms is not particularly unusual except that in this case Joe Webster did not have a family and was not a farmer. Joe was a 20-year-old college student studying economics and was my friend and roommate.

Joe was a methodical person, the son of a farmer. And although he did not want to farm for a living, enough of the blood was in him that he wanted to own a piece of land (as the saying goes, "You ain't no kind of man, if you ain't got land").

I have no idea how he got enough money together for a down payment to buy 80 acres nor do I remember being particularly interested. After all, I was in college too, and had far more pressing things to think about (girls). Our mutual friend Mike explained Joe's purchase with a shrug. "He's rich."

Well…not really. You see, I had visited Joe's folks' house a few times. The house was nice enough, only a few years old, but nothing like a mansion. What Joe talked about was not the amenities or square footage, but how his dad had planned and put money aside before the purchase.

At the time I knew very little about houses and even less about tractors, I just saw several brand-new John Deere tractors sparkling in the shed. Only later on another trip, when another friend of mine went along, did I find out that those tractors were between 15 and 25 years old and only looked new.

"Joe's dad must really know how to take care of machinery." I also learned that the tractors were not as big and powerful as others on neighboring farms, that the decision to get the old stuff was made carefully, weighing the pros and cons, measuring the benefits against the risks.

. . .

"You ain't no kind of man, if you ain't got land."

Measured. The whole family was like that. Joe's mom was a home economics teacher who served an omelet out of a pan, slicing it out like a pie, placing it on small plates next to two slices of cantaloupe, a bowl of oatmeal and a small glass of orange juice.

I remembered looking at the omelet pan with dismay. The other guest from college whispered in my ear, "I could eat that whole thing myself." But that was how they were; they didn't seem to do anything without measuring.

So that's when I got the idea that Joe wasn't rich—he was measured. Ever since he was a kid Joe earned money on the farm helping his dad, thinking, measuring and spending with slow methodical care.

If you're into investments, you can easily see that Joe could have made much more profitable investments over the years than farm land—and you will have missed the point.

If you save methodically out of your income, it does not really matter how you invest it. Most of the hard work is done when you save, not how you save.

After college, Joe got a job in the banking industry. The salary was good, but he got a roommate anyway, to split the rent. He could have gotten a new car but didn't. He kept driving an old but meticulously maintained Volvo.

I have no idea how Joe is doing today financially. We still stay in touch and, just like in college, he's not the type to share his finances, because he doesn't like to show off and it's none of my business.

His house is nice, but certainly not a mansion. It's the same one he bought when he first got married. I'm sure it was a bit crowded when the kids were younger, but they're gone now so it's plenty big. He and his wife travel once or twice a year. He has troubles, as we all do, but money is not one of them.

Someday, probably 50 years from now when Joe is dead and gone, they may start calling the 80 acres the Webster Place. And to anyone driving by, it won't look much different than the other farm fields.

But now you understand the difference.

SUCCESS SKILL

Delaying gratification is one of the great skills that successful people master.

housing

What kills a budget is not the little stuff. It's the big stuff.

Yes, I know that lattes and pizzas add up, but housing and transportation are the big items to crack first. Housing is easy when you're starting out: You have a quarter of your gross salary to spend on all things housing-related. That's it.

If you get a roommate (or two!) you can put the extra saved money aside for your house. Don't even look at houses until you have 20 percent of the cost of the house saved up for a down payment.

I know, I know...hardly anybody does that—only rich, retired people do that.

BODY

Dr. Physique

Some people look younger than they really are and Gene was one of them.

With an athletic build and no gray hair, he looked easily 20 years younger than his true age until his late 60s.

What caught up with him was the chocolate. And ice cream. And sweet rolls. Gene admitted that he had a sweet tooth. He'd had it all his life, but because he also enjoyed physical exercise, the sweet treats never seemed to affect his physique.

"I play racquetball five times a week. Never miss." The best way to eat sweets is to burn off the calories afterwards and that's what he did for quite a few years.

. . .

I play racquetball five times a week. Never miss.

Then Murphy's Law showed up. At first it was neck surgery that took Gene out for a few months. By the time he got back on the courts, he had to play a little catch-up.

Then his wife developed an illness and she needed care, so he decided to spend more time with her. And the early mornings at the racquetball court became later and more haphazard after he retired.

Out-of-town trips made it hard to keep a regular schedule with his old partners, other regulars retired from the game altogether and younger players were looking for a faster, more competitive game.

When I last saw Gene he was with his family, enjoying an evening out. There was a big serving of dessert on his plate, and he was about 40 pounds over the line. He finally looked his age. I can't say why exactly, but the sweets haven't helped much.

BODY

The Mountain Climber

Don was my friend's dad. I was more than a little scared of him.

He had a deep, loud voice and always seemed to be in a hurry. And he was big. Kind of looked like Hercules.

My friend loved to boast about his dad's physical prowess.

Back in the day, when his dad was still in boot camp, the drill sergeant said no one could do a certain number of mountain climbers, and Don was a cocky young kid and said he could.

Before I go any further, a mountain climber is like running in place with your hands on your head. Only with each step, you had to kneel down and touch your knee to the ground, then leap up, switch legs and touch the other knee. And so on.

If I told you that Don did 1,200 mountain climbers, would that be my faulty memory, or my friend's boastful exaggeration? All I know is the cocky kid put the drill sergeant in his place. And years later, that's why Don's knees still bother him today.

. . .

Don was my friend's dad.
I was more than a little scared of him.

This is the same man who was so powerful that when his Case tractor got stuck, he tried to heave the front wheels out of the mud. Which hurt his back.

My dad ran into him years later, when Don was in his 70s. He had long-since moved away, but he and dad had a good time catching up on the old days.

Dad said he didn't move too well and was using a walker.

BODY

Warren Buffett's Trick Question

I've heard Warren Buffet speak on this very subject and it's kind of a dirty trick, really. The richest guy on earth speaks to a group of high school students and asks them what kind of brand new car would they like.

I mean if I asked, they would get that it's a hypothetical question, but from him? Well, who knows?

Warren cautions that if they get this car they have to take care of it, because it's the only car they will get and it has to last the rest of their lives.

You can see the class thinking this over. Sounds like a good deal. Seems fair.

Then Warren lets the other shoe drop. No, I'm not giving you a car and, yes, you will own several cars in your lifetime. But you will only get one body, and if it's to last, you must take care of it.

I can't decide if the story works better coming straight from Warren Buffet or if they leave the room feeling slightly betrayed.

But for right now, you have a body that is pretty new—not too many dents and it probably even gets a few admiring glances as you cruise by. Enjoy it, but remember—it's the only one you'll get, and it has to last the rest of your life.

. . .

The richest guy on earth speaks
to a group of high school students and asks
them what kind of brand new car would they like.

BODY

Grandpa and the Eye-Rollers

My grandpa was an electrical engineer back in the day. For him that meant finding area farmers who needed help with lights, motors, electric machinery and, of course, pumps.

Well pumps, irrigation pumps, milking pumps—he knew how to calculate proper size, proper pipe diameter, whether to push the water uphill or pull it uphill and more. It's trickier than you think, which is what the guys at the hardware store were talking about.

We were at the hardware store; Grandpa was 88 and I was 24, along for the ride as he stopped to pick up something.

The hardware store employee was trying to help a customer who was having problems with his irrigation pump.

My grandpa saw the box with the pump illustration on the side, "You fellas got a question about a pump?"

...

They were not going to ask some deaf old guy a question about a pump. I could see their eyes rolling—they didn't even try to hide it.

They looked at each other and the old man in front of them.

"He's got a pump that's got a water hammer."

"What?" Grandpa was hard of hearing.

And that was it. They were not going to ask some deaf old guy a question about a pump. I could see their eyes rolling—they didn't even try to hide it.

Even my grandpa saw it. He got a little miffed and told them he had installed half the pumps in Whiteside County, and if they didn't know about installing an air tank to protect the pump from the pneumatic pounding the water would give it, then they could take their water hammer and pound sand.

I don't even think they were listening. It was as though his deafness made them unable to hear. I was as mad as my grandpa. Most of his hearing was lost as an artillery officer in the National Guard and during his service in World War II. And standing next to loud machinery.

Me, I never joined the National Guard, but I did mow the lawn and work in my shop. Later that month I bought myself a set of ear protectors. They were pretty bulky back then and I'm sure I got a few looks. I still use ear plugs and avoid loud concerts. I'm kind of a nut about it.

Now you know why.

BODY

The Donut Man

When I met the Donut Man he was at a sweetheart dance—the kind they give at senior centers for people celebrating 50 or more years of marriage. Folks would bring in their wedding photos and you had to guess who was who, which was tougher than you think.

He was about 80, a man with watery blue eyes and little expression. His most noticeable feature was his thickness. Yes, he was carrying some extra weight. But he was a thick person. Thick chest, thick forearms, thick fingers.

"I was a laborer. Mostly houses. We did everything back then—framework, plastering, wiring, plumbing, siding, roofing, the whole works, and I was the one who carried most of it."

"These heavy flatbed trucks would need some weight in the back for traction when they were running an empty load. They'd have these 500-pound weights riding on the back about yay high." He motioned with his hand up around his belly.

"Fellas wouldn't believe it, so for a quarter, I'd lift one off the ground and put it on the back of the truck." I imagined what that would look like—a solid trapezoid of steel with a cast handle in the top like you see at strongman shows.

Or 11 of those 45-pound plates they use in the gym stacked on the floor. Yikes.

"Then later I worked at a bakery. It was my job to load pallets of donuts onto the trucks."

"A pallet is a plastic rack, about two-and-a-half-feet square, and would hold about 10 dozen donuts," he explained. "They'd stack them on a stainless steel table about shoulder high. I'd hoist them on my shoulder and swing them around onto the trucks for delivery. All that twisting really worked the stomach muscles. They'd stack about 12 or 13 pallets just to see me do it."

I was figuring in my head about 15 to 20 pounds a pallet and started to see what he was talking about.

"I got appendicitis and they had to operate," he continued. "The surgeon stuck around to see me after I recovered. He was curious what I did for a living. I told him I worked in a bakery and he said he had to cut through one-and-three-quarters of an inch worth of stomach muscle just to get to my abdominal cavity—said he never saw anything like it."

It was pretty amazing stuff. I saw his wedding picture and could see how it could be true. He looked like an ox stuffed into a suit. His wife was a frail and petite thing. She was dressed up for the sweetheart dance; he was not.

I asked if he was going to dance and he shook his head. "I got arthritis all up and down my back, can't hardly move. All those years of lifting heavy things did me in."

LIFE LESSON

Injuries don't heal,
they just wait until you get older

→

cells are not equal

Muscle cells are made and repaired every day, your whole life long.

But cartilage must last. Like tread on a tire, when cartilage is gone, it's gone.

And when it's gone, your life literally becomes much more painful.

BODY

Double-Pump Burpees

I visit a young man in prison. He's got time on his hands. He and his four buddies do knee-bend ladders.

Each person does one deep knee bend, then each person does two, then three, and so on, until they are each doing 15 deep knee bends. Once they reach that, they head back down the ladder until they reach one.

My knees hurt just thinking about it. "How many is that?"

"I'm not sure."

Well I am, because I went back home and did the math. They each do 225 deep knee bends.

Per set.

"Per set?" I am now somewhat alarmed at just how many knee bends this kid is doing.

"We do ten sets a day." That's 2,250 deep knee bends a day.

"And then we do double-pump burpees." This same group does 12 sets of 100 double-pump burpees per day. Like I say, they have time on their hands.

This kid has put on 30 pounds of muscle just by doing ridiculous amounts of calisthenics.

I nod and I remember. "We used to do stuff like that, too. Doing push-ups through a deck of cards, the number on the card was the number of push-ups you did. I can't do that anymore."

. . .

12 sets of 100 double-pump burpees per day. Like I say, they have time on their hands.

"Why?"

"I hurt my wrists. Every time I do a push-up, my wrists ache the rest of the day."

"How did you hurt them?" he said.

"By doing push-ups."

BODY

Coach G and Coach S

If you are blessed to have one in your school, make sure your kid gets him or her, no matter what they're coaching—chess, choir, basketball, it doesn't matter. These people can teach skills and enthusiasm that change lives.

Coach G's thing was running. I don't imagine he weighed more than a buck thirty. Lean and tan, he'd be out with his teams, boys and girls, clip-clip-clipping along, with no apparent effort.

He almost made it to 90, and from what I saw he got along pretty well, right up to the end. If you're 5'9" and 130 pounds and have an effortless, gliding stride like Coach G, you might have the same luck.

On the other hand, you may be more like Coach S. He was a good guy who did a lot for his small town. He didn't really look like a runner, but he kept at it and you had to admire his grit.

The whole town knew his routine: get up early, stretch out on his front lawn, then huff out a three-mile route. And then he'd flop down in his front yard and stretch it out again.

On this particular day, he seemed to be stretching out longer than normal, but it was a Saturday, so he could do as he pleased.

Towards evening a curious neighbor came over to see the dew collecting on poor Coach S's cold body. His heart must have given out at the very end of his run.

LIFE LESSON

There is as much damage to the heart of a marathon runner as to the heart of a sedentary person.

MIND

Stepping Off a Cliff

This guy is dead, I'm sure of it. I must have heard a million stories and they sort themselves into different categories in my mind.

This guy was an Austrian-born Jew who fled his homeland after the Nazis took over. He was very motivated to avenge his country and his heritage and by special permission was allowed to join the British Commandos, a very tough group of elite forces.

He was on a cliff, trying to traverse its width and avoid falling to death or injury, using all the hand holds and foot holds and tricks of the climbing trade. He was out in front of the line of recruits, when suddenly he came to a problem: there were no hand holds to grab on to—nothing.

The instructor (imagine one of those lanky, upper-crust Britishers, with boundless courage and a gift for understatement) came along behind, up and over and around the other recruits, fearless and impatient.

THE PRO TIP

Courage is more of a decision than an emotion.

. . .

"The trick here is to step off like there is a place to land.
Of course, there's nothing there at all, really.

The secret is believing it's there."

"Oh, this? Yes, I thought it might be this part, a bit tricky, this one."

With a quick step back next to the recruit, the instructor stepped past him on the 85-degree grade, right foot slipping straight down, left foot swinging rapidly past it and, bang!—right onto a small outcropping about 10 feet away.

"You see," he said, "the trick here is to step off like there is a place to land. Of course, there's nothing there at all, really. But by the time you realize it's not there, you're already past it. The secret is believing it's there."

MIND

The Two Delusional Old Ladies

When I talked to her, I could tell the first woman was just a little off. She was planning ahead, taking care of her funeral so her kids and grandkids wouldn't be fighting about it. Which is smart, because I can tell you from experience that when it is planned, there isn't much fighting and when it isn't planned, it can be a real mess.

Anyway, I start asking her about her life and, right away, a rapturous look crossed her face.

"It was wonderful!" she said. "I grew up on a small farm and each morning, I'd get up and help my papa feed the cows and gather the eggs. Then we'd walk five miles to our country school and pick wildflowers, and then we'd come home to a delicious supper and ride our pony across the fields and meadows."

"I tell my granddaughter about it. She's five, and she says, 'Oh Grandma, I wish I was alive with you then. We'd ride ponies and pick wildflowers and play games. We'd have so much fun!' And I say, 'Well, it would be nice, but there will never be such wonderful days as when I was a child.'"

I could see that because of when she was born, she had to have grown up in the middle of the Dust Bowl and the Great Depression. But to her, it was some sort of fairyland. She was definitely delusional.

The second woman I met about a week later. Similar need and remarkably similar background, but a slightly different story.

"I grew up in the middle of nowhere, on a small, hardscrabble farm. Each day was a fight for survival. I'd have to get up, help with the chores, then walk five miles to school in horrible weather, and then it was back home for more chores. It was miserable."

. . .

Do you have any fond memories? Birthdays, family gatherings, Christmas, maybe?

I looked at her birthplace and birthdate. As I said, remarkably similar. I couldn't help thinking about the other lady. So, I tried a little prodding.

"Do you have any fond memories? Birthdays, family gatherings, Christmas, maybe?"

The woman looked at me and her frown deepened as she thought. Then after a moment of consideration, she barked a short answer, "No!"

The first woman had no bad memories, the second woman had no good memories, yet they both essentially had the same life.

Which lady would you rather be?

you are what you remember

If delusional means not seeing things as they are, then I submit to you that we are all delusional. None of us has the capacity to sense, process and remember all the things that are happening everywhere.

We can't even remember the finite amount of data and events we encounter as individuals. In fact, we actively ignore and forget as much environmental noise as possible to maintain our sanity. The little bits of conversations, experiences and knowledge we do save literally become our life.

It's an astonishing thing to think about. You are what you remember you are; your life is what you remember you did.

TRUISM

If life were easy,
it wouldn't be as much fun.

good stuff or bad stuff

If that's the case, why do some people seem to dwell on the good stuff and live happy lives and others only remember the bad stuff and remain unhappy?

The most incredible thing about this is, that for the most part, it is not a trait you are born with, but a habit you form.

Here's a trick I've used that may help you as well—keep a Gratitude Journal. Every day at the same time and place, write down three things you are grateful for.

Sound easy? Here's the catch—you can never repeat yourself. Now it becomes tougher. You must actively seek and search out little things you might have overlooked, like the first robin in spring, the car starting, the smile from the teller at the bank.

There are four other tricks I use that also help, but if I gave you all five at once, you might not try any of them. This is a good one and a great way to start. And it works!

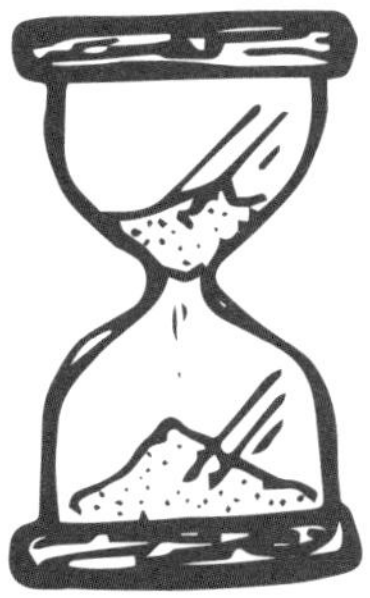

MIND

The Short Long Time

I was talking to a man in his early 20s who was agonizing about what he was supposed to do with his life. I was trying to get him to slow down a little bit, find something that he might like to try and see where it went.

"That's the trouble! I've been texting this guy about a job for a couple of weeks and he keeps putting me off!" he said.

I asked if he had been looking elsewhere, and he assured me that he had been relentlessly pursuing several opportunities…for just less than a month.

I looked at him and said: "If I were to ask you what a really long period of time was, what would you say?"

He pondered the question. He had never really thought about it. Finally, after weighing some sort of invisible scale in his mind, he nodded.

"Four months."

MONTH: february
TO DOs:
NOTES
INTERVIEW Friday @ 9:30 AM
POINTMENT
MINDER:
SAVE
- the -
DATE

LIFE LESSON

Our perception of time is shaped by how much of it we have.

. . .

"If I were to ask you what a really long period of time was, what would you say?"

MIND

The Day Starts at Nine

I see this guy usually in the morning. From a distance, he looks like he's 18—broad shoulders, slim hips, like a super hero using his secret identity.

He is what you might expect him to be: a fitness trainer.

As you get closer you see that you're wrong. He's probably in his late 20s, and when you get within a few feet, you see you're wrong again. He's probably in his 40s, clear-eyed, relaxed and focused, no matter how early the hour.

Must be one of those freaks of nature that only needs four hours of sleep.

Probably drinks steroids for breakfast.

Must be nice to be able to spend all day in the gym.

. . .

If you do the easy stuff, life is hard.
If you do the hard stuff, life is easy.

These are the thoughts of the envious. Then you find out a little more. He's married and has three kids. His wife stays at home, has some kind of chronic fatigue, and he is the sole bread-winner.

You find out he's trim because he never eats cakes, or sweets, or cheese pizza, or double burgers, or a rack of ribs, or any of the other things that you and I love to eat.

"My wife can't eat them because of her diet, so we all agreed we would stick with her." I wondered how that conversation went over with his kids. "No ice cream, kids, remember Mom is lactose intolerant." My initial theory that he is a genetic freak is fraying at the edges.

And if you look very closely, you notice other things. There is a slight stiffness to his walk, like he has some lingering pain, maybe a trick knee or worn cartilage.

If you happen to be around during the middle of the afternoon, you'll see him working out in a slow and focused manner, like the aging athlete he is, no flash or show, but the younger guys around the gym treat him with respect and consult on weights, and aches and stretches and treatments and exercises.

And the early riser bit?

"I owe these people my best. So, my day always starts at nine. PM. The night before. I need to have a good night's rest so I have the energy they need."

Oh.

He makes it look easy.

His answer is like his gaze—clear and to the point. If you do the easy stuff, life is hard. If you do the hard stuff, life is easy.

MEAT IS FOOD

MIND

The Eight-Year-Old Dad

Tom was a complex and fervent man. He could not stop shifting and moving. His voice would get louder as he talked and it could be embarrassing to be with him, since people could often easily hear him within a 40-foot radius.

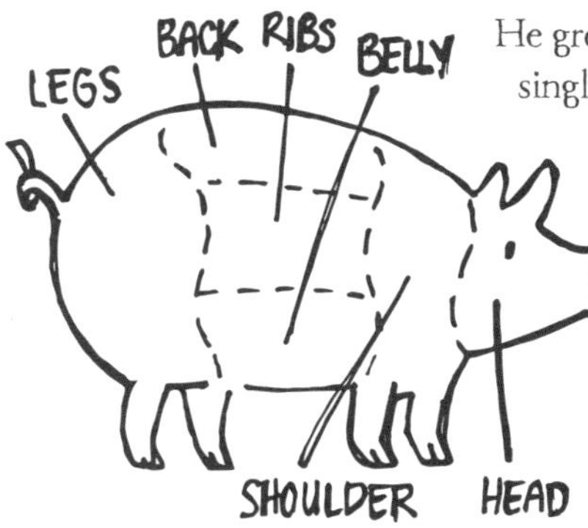

He grew up in the meat packing industry. His dad was a plant manager, so Tom was taught every single aspect of the industry, from the sausage plant to the kill floor, each job described in vivid, loud and lurid detail.

The job of killing animals and turning them into meat was his history and passion. I can still picture him talking about tying a long, sharp, double-edged blade to the middle finger of his right hand with a series of carefully wrapped loops of string, around and around until the blade (sharp enough to cut a scoop out of your arm if you weren't careful!) became an eight-inch extension of that finger.

Then, amidst the din of squealing hogs hanging from conveyor belts, he would reach, feel and—*snic-snac*—cut the jugular of each hanging hog, first one, then the next, then pulling and shifting levers until the lines of hanging hogs were moved and turned into lines of hanging meat.

It might seem gross to you, but it did not seem so to him, or to the men he worked with.

“Meat is food. And if you’ve ever been hungry, you know what I mean.” Tom’s words burn with memory. “My dad grew up in Oklahoma. When he was eight years old, his parents left town without him or his six-year-old brother.”
“What?” I am shocked at the story.

He nods, like he’s pointing to a vicious scar long healed over. “Yeah, it’s true. The two were abandoned. My father spent his youth hungry. Hungry, looking into the windows of groceries and restaurants at food he and his brother could not eat.”

“That’s why he got into meat packing—so he could eat and feed his brother.”

I sit and listen, trying to imagine what that might have felt like.

“When I was a kid growing up the most important thing to him was that I learn to work to eat,” Tom said. “And whenever there was a meal—breakfast, lunch or supper, he would ask each of us if we had enough to eat.”

“I guess I’m the way I am because of the way he was, and he was the way he was because of the way his dad was,” he reflected.

I wondered how many generations back that went.

ezekiel 18:2

“The parents eat sour grapes, and the children’s teeth are set on edge.”

MIND

The 23-Year-Old Mogul

I'm not sure how old Dan was. He could have been between 65 and 85. He had a certain…energy… that made it hard to focus on wrinkles or stature or movement, the things you usually use to determine age.

And his voice. It was large and commanding, not yelling, per se, but full and vibrant. He was a broadcaster. Of course. That explained the voice.

By the time I met him, he had bought and sold dozens of radio stations. Like a car dealer who loved to collect sheet metal, Dan would buy out of possibility, or profit, but always for love, too. He would declare, simply and with pride, "I'm a radio man." And he was a very successful radio man.

I could (and should) talk about the energy he brought into his later life, but for this time and story, I will talk about his early years and what happened long before I met him.

When he was 23.

"I used to come out here on weekends." He motioned to the general outdoors. We were in the Black Hills of South Dakota, a scenic place full of amazing natural beauty and crass tourist traps. He was the only person I met who could point to a radio tower in the distance and tell you the frequency, call letters and business history of the people, companies and corporations that had owned it since its construction.

It was while he was describing the lineage of one of these towers that he mentioned his weekend visits.

"Why did you come out here?" I asked.

"Oh, to dream, I guess." Dan seemed dismissive, almost embarrassed.

"Dream? About what?"

"I was a kid," he said. "I started working in radio when I was in high school, part-time. I went to college, but I couldn't get radio out of my blood, so I quit school and started in. On my weekends off,

I used to rent a little cabin and sit and plan my future. Set goals and stuff."

"How old were you then?"

"23," he said.

I know what I did with my weekends when I was 23.

Maybe that explains the difference.

MIND

The Project Man

Mark served in a military hospital, helping train orderlies when they arrived and preparing them for civilian life when they left.

Some were easy and some were projects.

Clarence was one of those projects. He had done his tour of duty and was going back home. Mark was helping him with the transition.

"It'll be easy, Top" ("Top" is a term of respect and endearment for the rank). "I got a brother-in-law back home who'll let me stay at his place for a couple weeks while I work at the factory. He says he can get me nights at first. Then when I get enough saved I'll be set."

Mark knew Clarence was smart, very smart. "Have you thought about the GI Bill, maybe going to college?"

Clarence laughed scornfully. "College? Me? You don't understand. I am a black man from the projects of Chicago. I will never go to college."

Well, Mark had some training using hypnosis in therapy, so he tried a little something.

. . .

Who you think you are is greatly impacted by what you were told.

"Clarence, I don't know who lied to you back when you were a kid, but I think it's time to get you to the truth."

He got a teddy bear and asked Clarence to go back to when he was a little boy. "Clarence, repeat after me: I am a smart, loving and good little boy and I can be whatever I want to be in this world."

At first, Clarence would only repeat what Mike suggested to him, but over time, under hypnosis, Mark would hear him arguing with his sisters: "I can too be whatever I want!" Maybe it was working.

One month later, Clarence left, promising Mark he would give college a try and that he would check back when he got there.

Enrollment time came and left. Mark heard nothing. One month later—nothing. Two, three months—still nothing.

Finally a letter came.

Now, 30 years later, Clarence is a law professor. I wonder what his sisters think about that?

Who you think you are is greatly impacted by what you were told.

"Two men looked out the same prison bars;
one saw mud, the other saw stars."

Dale Carnegie

The Man Who Was Comfortably Numb

The guy who died liked Pink Floyd. I mean *loved* Pink Floyd.

He worked in the trades. His service folder at the funeral showed a big guy with sunglasses and a frown.

"He sure loved Pink Floyd." His nephew came in to visit with me and talk about the funeral. "From the time he got up in the morning until he went to bed at night, all he listened to was Pink Floyd's *The Wall.* I thought he might have been exaggerating, but no—all day long he listened to that album.

Yikes!

I mean, have you listened to *The Wall*? It's a great album, maybe even a favorite of mine, but not all day long. It's pretty easy to see that Roger Waters doesn't like his fellow man very much, and after an hour or so of listening to the album, I don't like myself very much either.

. . .

After an hour or so of listening to the album, I don't like myself very much either.

But this guy, it was all he listened to. The back of his folder even had the words to "Comfortably Numb" written on the back. Look them up sometime. Not a very cheery send-off.

The nephew once joked with his uncle, "Jeez, aren't you worried about wearing this CD out?"

The uncle didn't say a word, he just pointed to the glove box. Inside were two new Pink Floyd *The Wall* CDs, still in the cellophane, waiting.

I can't remember how he died. Cancer, I think. He was in his early 50s.

if you frown all day

It's always been thought that emotions drive facial expressions.

But, recently, psychologists have tried some clever experiments that prove that the opposite also is true.

If you frown all day, you will feel measurably more sad. If you smile all day,
you will gradually feel happier. And it works for posture as well.
When it comes to your attitude, you are not only inside out, you are outside in.

now what?

If life is a journey, you and I traveled together for a while, as you read this book.
I've told you stories and pointed out events and people I've encountered along the way.

I hope my words have brought you some wisdom, possibly some warnings and some encouragement.
And I hope that you, in turn, will share insights with fellow travelers that may lighten their load.

COMING SOON!

Watch for I Like That Story, Book 2. Geared for folks ages 25 through 50, it contains a second helping of insights, inspiration, lessons and humor.

. . .

Visit ILikeThatStory.net

You'll find more stories on my website, in the form of blog posts, podcasts, radio shows and more. In addition, I speak to groups, companies and organizations nationwide.

You can reach me at jeff@ILikeThatStory.net

Jeff